W9-CMR-756

Tiptoe Into
SCARY PLACES

HAUNTED
AMUSEMENT PARKS

by Rachel Anne Cantor

Consultant: Ursula Bielski
Author and Paranormal Researcher
Founder of Chicago Hauntings, Inc.

BEARPORT
PUBLISHING

New York, New York

Credits

Cover, © Alexey Repka/Shutterstock; TOC, © Hellen Sergeyeva/Shutterstock; 4–5, © EnolaBrain81/Shutterstock, © Stefan90/iStock, © ladyenvy09/iStock, and © dragunov/Shutterstock; 6, © Jarretera/Shutterstock; 7, © Dean Jeffery; 8, © Roman Nerud/Shutterstock; 9, © AP Photo/The Charleston Gazette, Lawrence Pierce; 10–11, © Sean Pavone/Shutterstock; 10, © Mandias/CC BY-NC-ND-4.0; 11, © Soare Cecilia Corina/Shutterstock; 12–13, © Mandias/CC BY-NC-ND-4.0; 14, © lemonfluffy/Shutterstock; 15, © Niagara Falls (Ontario) Public Library; 16L, © life_in_a_pixel/Shutterstock; 16R, © Elzbieta Sekowska/Shutterstock; 17, © Cosmo Condina North America/Alamy; 18L, © Mike Hesp/Alamy; 18R, © seeshooteatrepeat/Shutterstock; 19, © Lario Tus/Shutterstock; 20, © fstopphotography/iStock; 21, © seeshooteatrepeat/Shutterstock; 23, © Pgiam/iStock.

Publisher: Kenn Goin
Editor: Jessica Rudolph
Creative Director: Spencer Brinker
Photo Researcher: Thomas Persano
Cover: Kim Jones

Library of Congress Cataloging-in-Publication Data

Names: Cantor, Rachel Anne, author.
Title: Haunted amusement parks / by Rachel Anne Cantor.
Description: New York, New York : Bearport Publishing, [2017] | Series:
   Tiptoe into scary places | Audience: Age 5–8. |
   Includes bibliographical references and index.
Identifiers: LCCN 2016042369 (print) | LCCN 2016046455 (ebook) | ISBN
   9781684020508 (library) | ISBN 9781684021024 (ebook)
Subjects: LCSH: Haunted places—Juvenile literature. | Amusement
   parks—Miscellanea—Juvenile literature.
Classification: LCC BF1471 .C36 2017 (print) | LCC BF1471 (ebook) | DDC
   133.1/22—dc23
LC record available at https://lccn.loc.gov/2016042369

Copyright © 2017 Bearport Publishing Company, Inc. All rights reserved. No part of this publication may be reproduced in whole or in part, stored in any retrieval system, or transmitted in any form or by any means, electronic, mechanical, photocopying, recording, or otherwise, without written permission from the publisher.

For more information, write to Bearport Publishing Company, Inc., 45 West 21st Street, Suite 3B, New York, New York 10010. Printed in the United States of America.

10 9 8 7 6 5 4 3 2 1

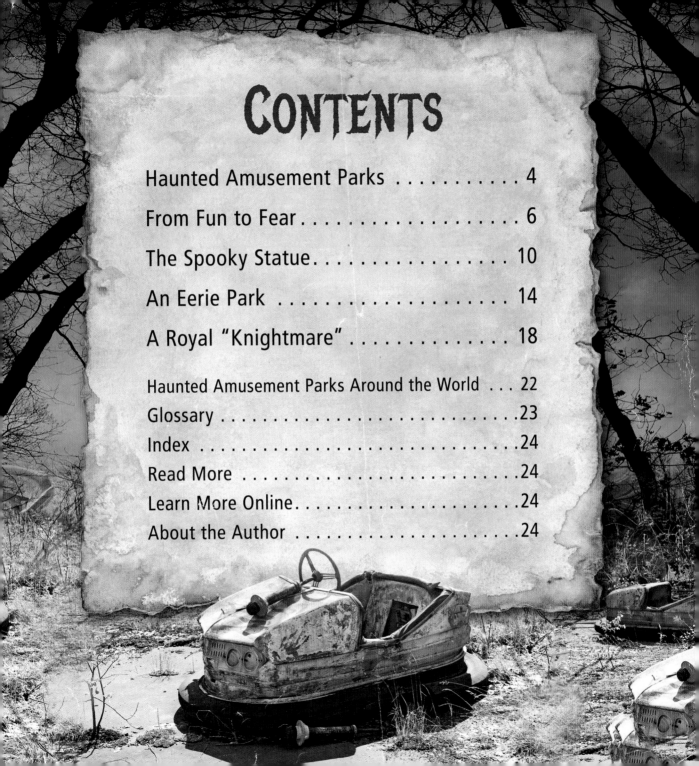

CONTENTS

Haunted Amusement Parks

You walk through a **deserted** amusement park. Although it was a place built for fun, you feel only fear. Thick vines grip a roller coaster track. The glass eyes of the merry-go-round horses stare at you. Suddenly, a low creaking sound breaks the silence. Is it the wind pushing one of the rides? Or could it be something else?

Get ready to read four spooky tales
about haunted amusement parks.
Turn the page . . . if you have the nerve!

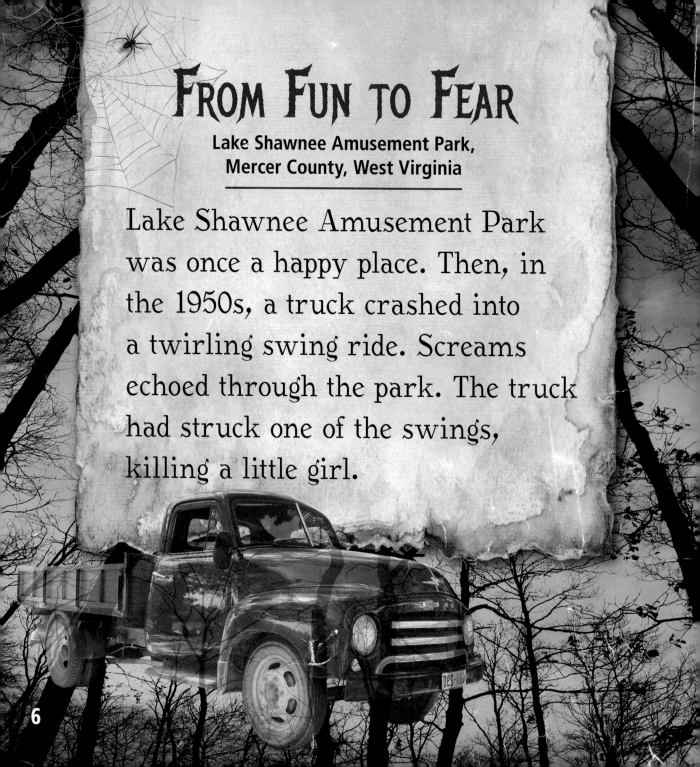

FROM FUN TO FEAR

**Lake Shawnee Amusement Park,
Mercer County, West Virginia**

Lake Shawnee Amusement Park was once a happy place. Then, in the 1950s, a truck crashed into a twirling swing ride. Screams echoed through the park. The truck had struck one of the swings, killing a little girl.

Today, the park is shut down. Tangled weeds cover the old rides. A rusted Ferris wheel looms in the sky.

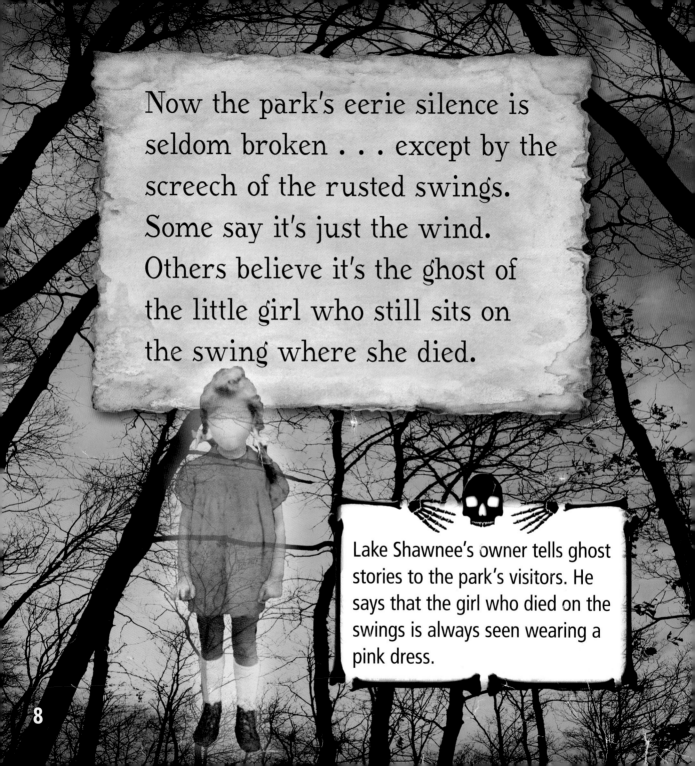

Now the park's eerie silence is seldom broken . . . except by the screech of the rusted swings. Some say it's just the wind. Others believe it's the ghost of the little girl who still sits on the swing where she died.

Lake Shawnee's owner tells ghost stories to the park's visitors. He says that the girl who died on the swings is always seen wearing a pink dress.

8

9

THE SPOOKY STATUE

Gulliver's Kingdom, Kamikuishiki, Japan

In 1997, Gulliver's Kingdom was built near a mysterious forest. People say that ghosts of the dead wander the dark woods. Maybe the park was doomed from the beginning.

Gulliver statue

The park was based on the book *Gulliver's Travels*. In the story, the main character, Gulliver, goes to a place where tiny people live. They capture him and tie him down. The park had a huge 147.5-foot-long (45 m) statue that showed Gulliver tied up.

Gulliver's Kingdom had few rides. Most visitors just walked around and looked at the giant statue. Its empty eyes seemed to gaze back.

Then, in 2001, Gulliver's Kingdom closed. That's when people came to **vandalize** the park. Soon, the statue started to **rot.** Gulliver began to look like a huge **corpse** lying near the haunted forest. In 2007, the spooky park was torn down. Was it **cursed** from the start?

An Eerie Park

Erie Beach Amusement Park, Ontario, Canada

In 1928, people were flocking to
Erie Beach Amusement Park.
Visitors enjoyed rides like the
Flying Ponies merry-go-round and
the Wildcat roller coaster. Then a
depression hit. Many people
lost their jobs.

Few could afford the fun of
Erie Beach. The park closed
in 1930, and the rides
began to fall apart.

When the park closed, people still came to see the crumbling remains. However, they were in for a shock. They also saw ghosts!

15

Just before the park closed down, a boy died there. He had fallen out of a boat on a water ride and drowned. It was a terrible **tragedy**. Some visitors to the park have seen his ghost. His **spirit** seems to be forever trapped at Erie Beach.

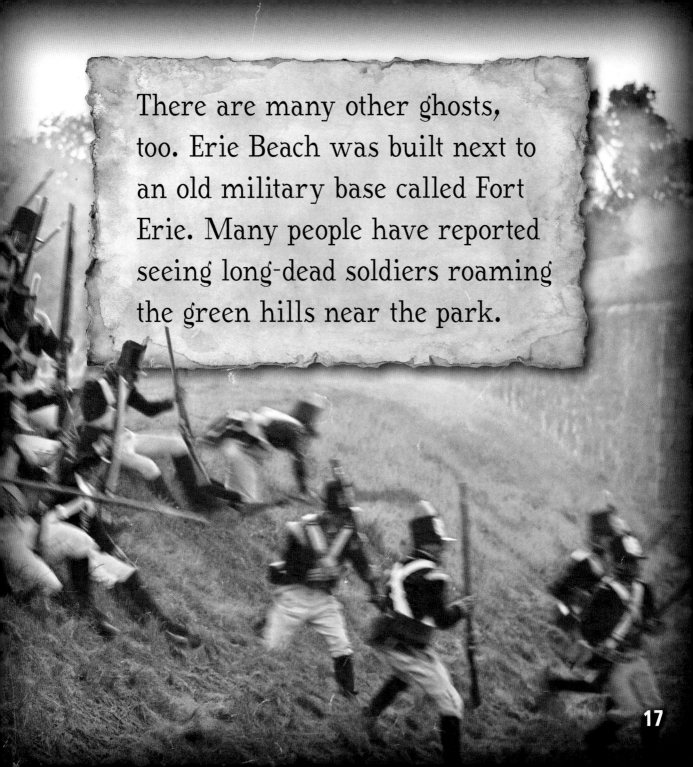

There are many other ghosts, too. Erie Beach was built next to an old military base called Fort Erie. Many people have reported seeing long-dead soldiers roaming the green hills near the park.

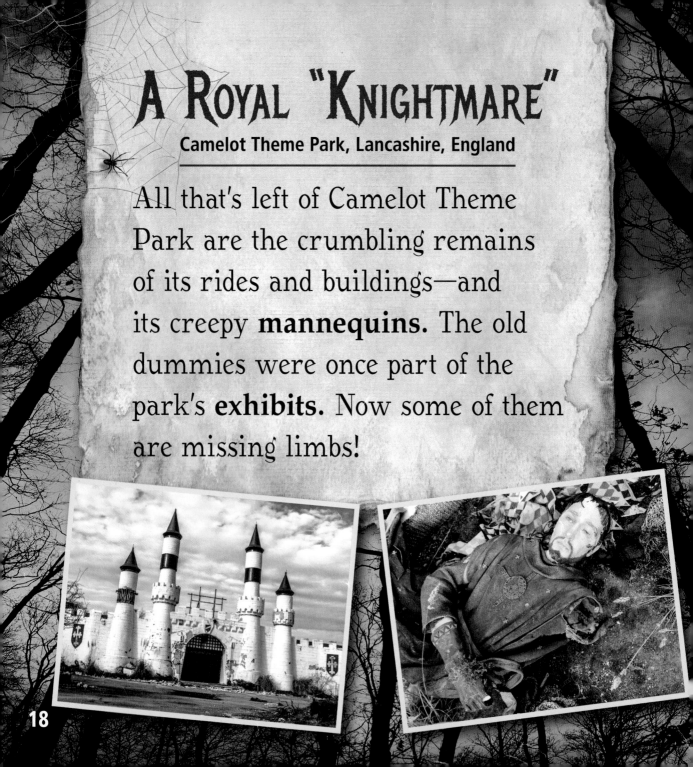

A Royal "Knightmare"

Camelot Theme Park, Lancashire, England

All that's left of Camelot Theme Park are the crumbling remains of its rides and buildings—and its creepy **mannequins.** The old dummies were once part of the park's **exhibits.** Now some of them are missing limbs!

According to **legend**, a powerful magician once lived in a lake called Martin Mere. The lake was drained, and a park was built in its place in 1983. The park had a **medieval** theme, with castles and sword fights. It also had a giant rollercoaster.

At first, visitors flocked to the Knightmare roller coaster and other rides. Then, all of a sudden, people stopped coming. By 2012, the park had to close. The broken-down rides and mannequins now sit eerily silent—looking like a true nightmare.

What kept visitors away? Perhaps the park failed because a curse had been placed on it by the magician of the lake.

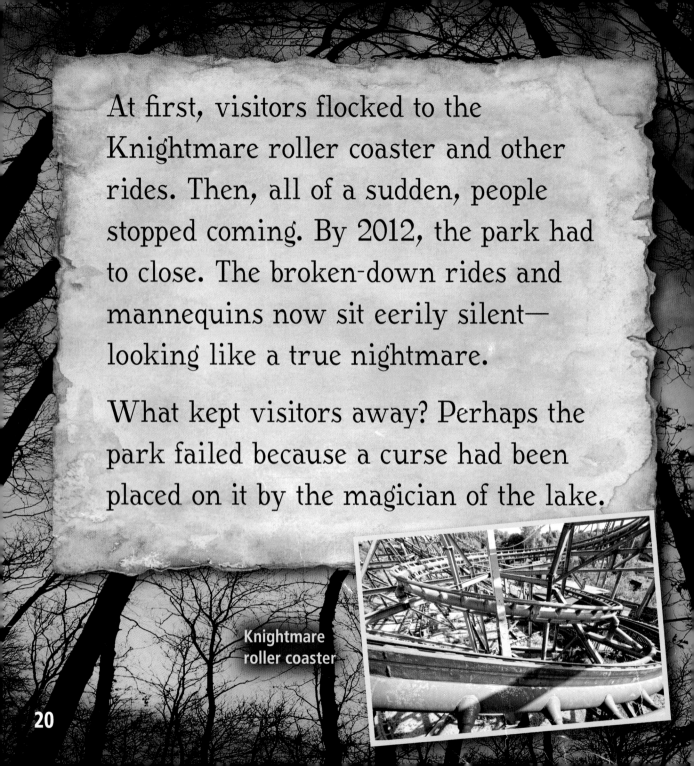

Knightmare roller coaster

No one knows who destroyed the frightening mannequins or why.

HAUNTED AMUSEMENT PARKS
AROUND THE WORLD

ERIE BEACH AMUSEMENT PARK

Ontario, Canada

Check out the spirits of soldiers who wander this abandoned amusement park.

LAKE SHAWNEE AMUSEMENT PARK

Mercer County, West Virginia

Visit the ghost of a little girl who haunts a swing ride.

CAMELOT THEME PARK

Lancashire, England

Did the magician of the lake curse this theme park?

GULLIVER'S KINGDOM

Kamikuishiki, Japan

A giant statue was built near a haunted forest.

Arctic Ocean

NORTH AMERICA

EUROPE

ASIA

Atlantic Ocean

AFRICA

Pacific Ocean

Pacific Ocean

SOUTH AMERICA

Indian Ocean

N

W E

S

Atlantic Ocean

AUSTRALIA

Southern Ocean

ANTARCTICA

GLOSSARY

corpse (KORPS) a dead body

cursed (KURST) under an evil spell and therefore likely to experience misfortune

depression (di-PRESH-uhn) a time when many people lose their jobs, businesses, or homes, or become poor

deserted (de-ZUR-tid) left empty or alone

exhibits (eg-ZIB-its) presentations or displays shown to many people

legend (LEJ-uhnd) a story handed down from long ago that may be based on fact but is not always completely true

mannequins (MAN-uh-kinz) life-size models of people; dummies

medieval (meh-DEE-vuhl) from the time of the Middle Ages, around the 400s through the 1400s

rot (RAHT) to decay and fall apart

spirit (SPIHR-it) a supernatural being, such as a ghost

tragedy (TRAJ-uh-dee) a terrible event that causes great sadness or suffering

vandalize (VAN-duh-lyze) to destroy or damage property on purpose

Index

Read More

Hoberman, Mary Ann. *You Read to Me, I'll Read to You: Very Short Scary Tales to Read Together.* New York: Little, Brown and Co. (2007).

Teitelbaum, Michael. *The Doomed Amusement Park (Cold Whispers).* New York: Bearport (2016).

Learn More Online

To learn more about haunted amusement parks, visit:
www.bearportpublishing.com/Tiptoe

About the Author

Rachel Anne Cantor is a writer who grew up in New Jersey and lives in Massachusetts. She loves going to amusement parks but hasn't spotted any ghosts . . . yet.

FREDERICK COUNTY PUBLIC LIBRARIES

JUL 2017

2 1982 02928 7590